JAN
1

JAN
1

Be My
Valentine

Be My Valentine

HAPPY
EASTER

HAPPY
EASTER

Happy
Mother's
Day

Happy Mother's Day

HAPPY
FATHER'S
DAY

HAPPY
FATHER'S
DAY

TRICK
OR
TREAT

TRICK
OR
TREAT

Season's
Greetings

Season's
Greetings

Happy
Birthday

Happy
Birthday